# BARNEY GOOGLE AND SNUFFY SMITH

*by Fred Lasswell*

TEMPO BOOKS, NEW YORK

BARNEY GOOGLE AND SNUFFY SMITH

A Tempo Book/published by arrangement with
King Features Syndicate, Inc.

PRINTING HISTORY
Tempo edition / October 1977
Second printing / March 1983

All rights reserved.
Copyright © 1969, 1977 by King Features Syndicate, Inc.
This book may not be reproduced in whole
or in part, by mimeograph or any other means,
without permission. For information address: Tempo Books,
200 Madison Avenue, New York, N.Y. 10016

ISBN: 0-448-15683-0

Tempo Books are published by Charter Communications, Inc.
200 Madison Avenue, New York, New York 10016.
Tempo Books are registered in the United States Patent Office.
PRINTED IN THE UNITED STATES OF AMERICA